CHAIR IN THE DESERT

Chair in the Desert

4/15/04

poems by

Richard Chess

FOR EMILY WARN —

DRINKING FROM MIRIAM'S WELL!

PEACE,
Rick

🏛 UNIVERSITY OF TAMPA PRESS • TAMPA, FLORIDA • 2000

Manufactured in the United States of America
Printed on acid-free paper
First Edition

The University of Tampa Press
401 West Kennedy Boulevard
Tampa, FL 33606

ISBN 1-879852-67-5

Library of Congress Cataloging-in-Publication Data

Chess, Richard.
  Chair in the desert : poems / by Richard Chess.
    p. cm.
  ISBN 1-879852-67-5 (alk. paper)
  I. Title.
  PS3553.H42 C48 2000
  811'.54--dc21

00-010167

Contents

IV. from the *Elul* Notebooks

V. Broken Vessels

For Laurie
and for Alice, Margaret, and Gabe

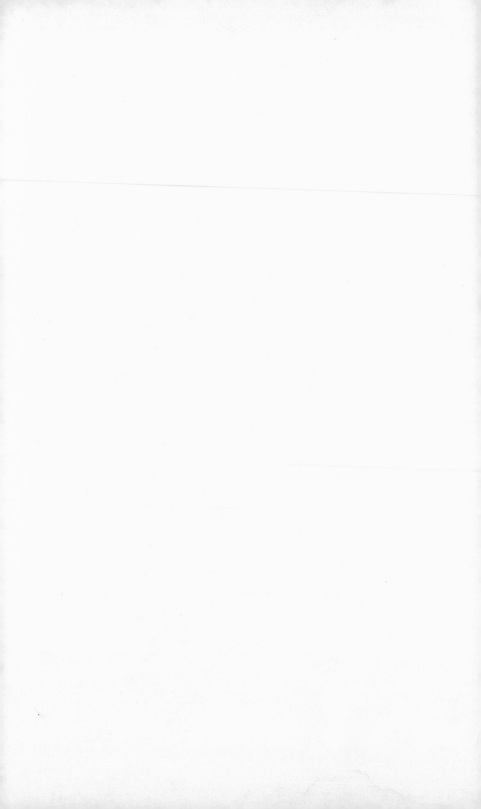

I. Waking in *Elul*

Elul: Preceding the ten days of penitence, the Jewish month of *Elul* is a period of repentance and of special ascetic and devotional practices. A rabbinic homily derives an allusion to the name of the month from the initial letters of *Ani le-Dodi ve-Dodi Li*, "I am my beloved's, and my beloved is mine," Song of Songs 6:3. The *shofar* is sounded daily at the morning service (except on the Sabbath), and Psalm 27 is recited. Rabbinic lore connects the special significance of *Elul* with the 40 days of Moses' stay on Mount Sinai (Exodus 34:28) which was calculated to have commenced on the first of *Elul* and ended on the 10th of *Tishri* (the Day of Atonement).

—Encyclopedia Judaica

Meditation upon Waking in *Elul*

I fear to open my lips to speak as I arise to pray.
I tremble as I rise to stand before the day.

I know the hours that will be granted me
could be handed to one who would fill them with deeds.

I know rivers praise you, I know wires
convey your charge to our homes.

From my window, I see the mountain
on which my house is heavy thought,

and I see the concentration of sun at this hour.
The end of creation's year draws near.

Across the valley, I hear gears,
smell oil, and understand

that work praises you, early work, yard work,
intellectual, house, and hard work.

I know my name is not among the names
you love. The fragrance of doubt

does not make you swoon. I have tasted
from a thousand tables—pine nut,

pickle, saffron, speckled trout, artichoke, oregano,
lamb, cream, peppercorn, wonton, rye, mold—

and I have been enchanted by voices
in woods and malls, cars, pools, spring and fall,

but this morning is a step on which I stand, knowing
not whether I rise toward a temple

or fall from it, my offering refused.
I am wrinkle and stain, so poor in deeds,

so lacking wisdom, which in this nation is money,
how can I perform the simple act

of walking gently, wisely, righteously today?

Leviticus for Daughters

Do not pierce your tongue.
Do not drive simply
    to speed up, slow down: the world
will not tolerate your setting your own pace.
Do not forget the song your mother sang.
Do not leave the table without a plate:
    a hand is designed to help.
Do not put a stumbling block before the blind, do not
    give away the answer to the student cheating behind you.
Do not pierce your bellybutton.
Do not use perfume
    or any product tested on animals.
Do not sleep late tomorrow, you need to
    complete the application.
Do not bring that boy into my house again.
Do not hate me or your father (wherever he rusts) or
    your little brother who stole the birthright from you.
Do not curse, do not curse
    the driver who cuts you off,
    the cashier who shortchanges you,
    the boy who betrays you, the player on the other team
    who jabs you in the back
    when you are standing to field the ball punted toward you—
we are not a people who live easily
among others, so we must live quietly
    on the street, in our seats.
Your body—don't paint it, it isn't canvas.
Don't use it as a ticket to admit you to the show.
Don't let just anyone stick his bill on it, his circular.
And don't let it think

for itself—that's how Shirley's daughter
    got into the mess she's in.
Don't pierce your nose, but if you do
    wear gold in the hole, don't
    ever melt it down
    like that weak generation lost in the desert.
You know that noise you hear coming
    from my bedroom before dawn? Don't you
be crazy like me.
Don't shave.
Don't eat your own blood. Be holy.
Don't forget the Sabbath—even
    when you are desecrating it.
Even if god is just a word, say it
    the way you say, when
    you're irate, forlorn,
    mother.

Klezmer

Daughter of a butcher, grandson of a wagon
    twin of the new moon—that's who this music is

though it was tortured, shot, drowned, gassed, butchered
though its gold teeth were extracted, its smile ironed out,
though its legs—how it danced from village to village to village
    with the rebbe in its arms—were broken
though its crystal was smashed, its baby tossed into the air to see if
       it really was a miracle
though there was a corner where it liked to meet
    in the afternoon to smoke and consider the news
        and women passing by
    before the women were shrunk to regulation sizes
    before the news was a colossal darkness
    before the smoke was all there was to eat
it didn't die, it didn't refuse to die, it didn't resist—it wasn't that brave
    or dumb—it didn't offer its body for experimentation
    it didn't collaborate, it just didn't stop
    wheezing and rattling—breathing!

listen to the accordion, how even with that guy squeezing the air
    out of it it still sings

listen to the clarinet, that delight—

related to mud, *up* goes down into a well and rises again, its face
    shining and sharp

at night, late, especially on the Sabbath
    we make shofar noises

early the next morning, too, before the mall
        awakens, a little groggy
an obscene and proud screw of sound
        coming from a Volkswagen that the ghost of our mother
spits on and blesses

it lives on air, the way poor musicians do (though that fiddler
        owns a posh condominium overlooking the Mediterranean)
it rides with birds and hail and light, its traveling companions
        —it's stopped at the border, it crosses—

maybe you hear it for the first time at the bar mitzvah of a
        neighbor's child
maybe you hear it for the first time on public radio, Chanukah,
        and you cry to your husband, chewing nails in front of the tv,
        the oil burns at the darkest hour of the year!

or maybe you hear it on stage, under a tent—
        your grandparents paid for the tickets
        and no one, not the wife or kids or your own pastel mother
        reminds you that *your* grandparents—just atoms now—
        were raised in South Philly on Mummers

or maybe you hear it in an alley in Safed, Israel,
        as it weeps from the window of a lover's loft, a mystic or
                artist there
in the afternoon, the hours when the study house is quiet, gallery
                locked,
        the sky yogurt-blue, same as the color of the headstones of
                giants of Kabbalah
        buried on the hillside just below your stroll

[16]

or maybe you've never heard it, not in your neighborhood
        meditation hall, courtroom or spa
not where you roll a cart with trays of food down a hall

or dip a wick in melted wax or squat in pain at the top of the stairs
or spit cherry pits into grass or sign a will in the presence of three
        witnesses

today klezmer is still being scraped from weeds and blown
        from windows of 5,000 destroyed villages

it's history in a spoon, it's our limp
it's the first language of our home, you could say
        if your food wasn't the hoagie
        if you weren't born with henna-colored palms
                in a village where goat roasts and musicians,
                not to violate the orthodox Muslim ban
                on musical instruments, bang on gasoline
                cans and brass tea trays, Yemenite soul

still the cry, still the crowd
        dipping, twirling, beating, smoking–
in a barn, study house, social hall, tables
        slammed aside
thousands under a July sky stepping up and
        down on a lawn

–can you keep up with mother's moods? –outrage, sorrow–
but mother, this is a wedding, we're supposed to be happy
        pleads the clarinet, this is the Messiah
        we're chuckling about here

Society Girl, Durham, NC, circa 1960

I couldn't date a Negro, right?
So I dated *him*. Far from his tribe,
his eyes invited me to explore
his people's history which he keeps
inside his body, in rooms dimly lit, drafty,
stinking of garlic, milk, and books,
the slaughterhouse Leviticus . . .

The band played "Mustang Sally."
We danced. When we dipped,
I knew he wouldn't drop me
to the dusty floor, just like I knew,
when he flung me toward the pearls
of heaven, he'd receive me,
when I returned to this echoing world,
like an angel in his arms.

Their village destroyed, his grandparents
fled through snow to ship
on which they coughed and bled
until it docked, near Liberty.
Then, admitted, ashore, they drifted south.

Late in his car, his universe
expanded to include me on the map
of bones he would uncover.

Once there were sacrifices.
Now there is prayer, which most do not sing.
The list of expulsions is long.

The names of the dead
as many as there are grains of sand, stars.
Once there were priests. Then rabbis.
Now owners of department stores.

Morning light waxing burley leaves,
I rose toward school on the hill.
I knew what to hide and what to show
the girls in the hall who would never
risk arousing a father from leather
comfort by an evening window.
See the neck, that's the kind mark they leave.
They fascinate and flatter.
They make your ears flutter
in the breeze of intelligence,
meanwhile unclasping the bra.
Then, the catalogued sins a dim recognition,
you part your lips to let out an *o*
of submission, first syllable
of a psalm of praise.

Though he's not black, he's
the closest I'll ever come
to thanking daddy
for dividing the world
into so many white and forbidden pieces.

II. I and Thou, Baby

I and Thou, Baby

> . . . *the moments of the Thou appear as strange lyric and dramatic*
> *episodes, seductive and magical, but tearing us away to dangerous*
> *extremes, loosening the well-tried context, leaving more questions*
> *than satisfaction behind them, shattering security . . .*
> —Martin Buber

The Essential Kabbalah

After a night with your red hair,
    the need to increase
aloneness woke me.
    Like stripping body from soul, I
left your bed, drove Kings
    Highway home.
Mother was sparkling
    in the community pool, father
revealing himself in the back room of the store.
    I was free to humiliate myself
anywhere in the house—
    in the ark of their bed,
on the kitchen's linoleum floor.
    Have you ever reduced yourself
so extremely
    that you weren't attached
to anyone, not even by a hair?
    Underwear down, I sat
on a wet bathroom mat and began
    to eliminate you, dream
or vision, from life. My desire
    was nineteen years old,
my eyes older: though it was a sunny June

morning in the window,
darkness spread over everything
    you were. You would have been
in the liquor closet by now
    with our boss, yours and mine,
taking stock, trembling
    over a case of gin.
Suddenly, my body, adorned
    with good deeds
as if fine balsam oil had been poured over it,
    head to feet, emanated bright light.
I had penetrated a thought: a new way
    to serve you.

                    *

Swingers

After I wrote my first love poem,
just as I was becoming aware
of events in your body (I still wasn't sure
where exactly to touch), we met
a sheriff and his wife at the pool.
He must have admired the ripple of your skin
when his joke was Tennessee.
I wasn't attentive to his art,
so I wasn't prepared, early that evening,
in their motel room, for his welcome:
Would you like a drink? Have a drink.
Shall we play cards? Let's play cards.
Let's sit on this big bed and play.
It would be untrue to say we were losers.
Her top off, his wife sat, bored,
while he worked you and I followed

to the loftiest peak. There, I saw you
casting away whatever girlish mysteries
had lived in you till then. The world
stands with its content of truth:
You were nineteen that night, burning
like a candle on a cake.

*

Photograph

If there were a picture of me that night,
would it reveal the skin of a young man
exhibiting and defining bright ways and gloom,
or the heart extended in space, stretching
from shore to sky, starlit sky into which a moon rises?
A camera could have captured that exact dream behind us.
After lamb, after cognac, you wanted more,
the whole stuff of life, so on a bench
on the inn's grounds, you lifted
the skirt, straddled me, and, certain
no one was passing by
on the path to the lake, urgent and tense
you seized and stuffed me inside,
then wrapped arms around my shudders.
I could have been any man
and you would have done the same.
Nothing more than history in your eyes,
I still believed the heart
enclosed us within its circle.

Would a snapshot show how much
I had lost by then, how much hair?

At 22, hair is an eternal strength.
Because we were careful
to resist the natural straining
toward expanding movement,
any witness to our true life at dusk
would have regarded what she observed
as apparent and illusory and continued strolling.
Fool, missing the great shudder, the holding
of breath, the shining
streaming constancy: what a photograph is.

*

Dishes

Where there is danger, I thought, there is a poem:
a plate to whiz by, if you didn't move, your right ear.

It's not exactly a blur to me, the garden
apartment where we engaged, so we believed,
in the universal struggle. Madly and unceasingly
hunted in an empty circle, you
cowered as I picked up everything fragile at hand.

The feverish world
outside—entirely yours now, the whole
complicated cock
and frenzy, hopping from one lover to another—
but inside, my feverish desire
to see you surrender
to a face of the earth, green and blue
kindness, my love.

You must remember it
differently, our trial
of the final darkness.

O, my ability to use
my whole being, I told the psychiatrist
when asked what I liked most about
myself.
You'd recommended him, a friend.
When I reported
his diagnosis—one-way love—
you accused me
of emptying
out the reality of our story.

Here's something real
I never told anyone:
one day while you worked
the lunch shift, I played
with your poodle, pretending
we were a carnival ride.
I was the steel
machine and she was the thrill-
seeker at the end of a leash
swinging around and
around in the air.
Just a dog,
she wouldn't have had any belief
in release.

Feelings

Do not describe, the therapist said
   when I tried to
describe the dress I bought for you
   with tips. A dress
from the hippest shop on South Street.
   No special occasion. Just
a way to win you over again.
   There is a *thing*, there is another
thing, the therapist said. Tell me
   what you felt that night
she drove to New York
   with the painter, the busboy
you both work with, what need
   isolated you in the den of your parents' house—
they slept soundly upstairs;
   your brothers, who knows
what sand they were tossing on, drunk
   or tripping, or what house
in the neighborhood they were breaking into
   during those long hours
when a tugged and dragged man says,
   I imagine something, I imagine
something, until gradually and suddenly
   the lust of the human race
is in that Beetle with them, your girlfriend
   and that gifted, serious, young painter
who introduced you to Rimbaud,
   and you are alone with the entertainment
console in the den
   while he manipulates her, exactly

as she instructs him, in the car by the river
	at an hour that belongs to things not people.
What I wouldn't say to him, I couldn't say
	to you, not early the next morning
when I cruised by your house,
	to which I still had a key (we were
still mingling and separating then).
	Parked in front of the house, his used car
had something to do with me.
	I'm not sure what I thought
I needed then, but
	the dress, your favorite, which I found
in the closet, rent easily.
	You wanna know how I felt?

*

Tripping

Tripping
terrified me
but not as much as thought.
You had already left
that part of self that lived
with me.
There I remained
enclosed in mystery:
a home that does not contain heaven.
That's why I'd agreed
to purple acid,
sweet, our friends agreed, a way out
of but not away from
suffering. First rush, the acid

burned into me and I
trembled and
surrendered
to the scale in which I was one
vibrating
note, you were another.
How we spent the day
doesn't really matter.
In poems men say too much.
It's our way of freeing ourselves
from isolated bodies.
If we go
on our way, our separate ways,
I thought
while lying on a small bridge.
We were looking up
at what we knew
would be the one true
blue sky of the year, at rest
in the eternal
middle of a question.

☆

Abortion

Afterward, I alone stayed to comfort you.
By then, we were nearly finished unraveling
the tangled incident of romance.
But on this day, a shade was to be drawn, a hand
placed on your brow.
We had had to drive an hour south
to the clinic in the shadow of the Delaware Memorial Bridge,
an hour in the heat of day back.

If there had been a jade flute in the house,
I would have played it to banish the eyes
of all your lovers watching.
Maybe you couldn't see them.
I wanted you to feel safe in the shelter of my presence.
I wanted to clasp the sun dress
draped over the back of the chair at the desk.
I sat by the bed reading poems, trying to
find my bearings.
As you sweated and slept, I waited,
easier than waiting at 2 a.m. for the sound of your powder
blue Beetle coming up the street.
I knew then that I could choose
to reside in feelings—despair, too, is interesting—
or I could plunge into the mystery
of my body separate from yours.
That's when you extended your hand, signaling for me to take it.
Holding it, an uneasy fluttering soul-bird,
I thought, tomorrow, when we part for good,
our parents will think:
put together, they did not create human life.

✽

Sudden Death

When I needed to get as far
away from my self as possible, I flew
to Jerusalem where I stuffed prayers
in the mouth of the Wall
hoping it would say my words next
time it spoke to God.

*

Waiting in the dark for a bus,
my reflection
in the window of a store.
I said, I see you, I see
my face, my kind.

*

One day, when a visitor from home said
your name, my canceled existence
was recalled.
From habit and obtuseness, I pictured myself
coming into contact with truth—
your body
swinging from heat
to cold, stranger to lover.
What brought me back: a blind
eye, Jerusalem's, raised
toward me.

*

The man I was at home
would have lengthened the fiction
of his special being
and dropped a coin in the beggar's cup, two coins.
I turned down one of the hundred paths
through a heart,
on some of which gods
and demons are at strife.

✣

Desire led me
but never to an encounter in which everything flamed.
Eventually, I was freed
from enchantment
but not saved.
This at least I knew: I was finished
with dying that lasts the span of a man's life.
There would be many sudden deaths for me,
any time I heard your voice
coming from another woman's mouth.

✣

I and Thou: *I and Thou, Baby*

What would I do without you, Buber, what would I do without
you? Without you I would not have met her here, wherever *here* is,
wherever memory dwells and works. Maybe she has been moving
toward me for years, following a slow subterranean course that, in
truth, does not exist. Maybe she has been waiting, not seeking to
recast me as a servant of former times. Weak and empty, I was
drawn into the orbit of your mastery from where, at pains to say
anything that would fill the heavens, I said merely what has
already been said of love. For example, *long ago, one night after work,/
down by the river, in a sleeping bag,/two great children, really,/in the bodies of
a man and a woman,/swallowed up every miracle the world had to offer/until,
illuminated and exhausted,/the bareness of the full moon shining/into their
bareness, they lay,/the scent of burnt-offering in the air around them.* When
we were together, my first love and I, I prayed that she would not
annihilate me. Now, thanks to a decision, purposive though
dimly seen, wholly mysterious, to skim *I and Thou*, we are together

again. I sacrifice my everyday hours—they pass like a streak of sun on a maple twig—to burn at my highest in her presence. Without you, Buber, I would not be able to say to myself, the only way I know to speak to her, *you know always in your heart that you need me more than anything.*

III. Temporary Resident

Home

You put the word in my mouth.
You put a dime in my pocket,
and added my name to the list of travelers,
and cleared the mind for good traveling.
You put the word in my mouth.

At the end of the day, my life
as your disciple was done.
You put the word in my mouth
and gave me a key and ignored
my claims of unworthiness.

You put the word in my mouth,
the dime in my pocket,
and pointed to the sea.
In my 21st year, I crossed it.
With father's arms, I paddled
and flew

till on the shore I was met by
mother's desire for me:
a daughter of Zion.
As if we had been reunited
after as many years as there were stars overhead,
we kissed on a slippery jetty,
we cried out the names of each
of our wounds.
I pulled off her skirt. I needed to
eat my history.
What the sun wouldn't say

when it finally appeared
in the sand, I said. *Because
you put the word in my mouth,
I say this is home.*

Paper Jerusalem

in the visitor's book
my pen makes a sound
like a ghost's from the ground

traveling because of the smell
of cinnamon
I cannot find the gateway to heaven
I cannot find an arrow

privilege of
the blind who behold
the Temple on high
the full moon

cleanliness
of a woman who adorns herself
but leaves something off
in remembrance of the night
she miscarried because of Titus

diaries boast
you will never get in here
the site named Adonai-Yireh

on the mount
of the Lord there is vision vision
kindled in one corner of the King's eye

Temporary Residence

Way Down

Once we slaved in the sun and slept
in the shadows of our labor. We gave
our daughters to their men and buried
our parents wherever
they fell and left the graves
unmarked. Thus unburdened, we moved
boulders without the heavy past
on our backs, the sorry future
on our chests. Those for whom we worked
worshipped the sun disk and paddled

slow boats across the ochre-tinted river.
Their fingernails shone like ripe
grain, their black hair
gleamed like onyx.
We ate hard bread and drank
goat milk and cursed
the ancestor who had obeyed
a voice in his mis-wired head
and led us there.

Desert Crossing: First Day

In the afterglow of what was given
in *Sivan*, we walk
on a scroll of land until the scroll ends,
where we wait and gaze
ahead, just beyond the tip

of the tongue, at that which is
called not *Israel*, exactly, or *ease*.
Why not settle here, where
one world dissolves
into another and what one
loves is not the crown
worn once, briefly, but the knowledge
that *deserve* has no say
in what one receives?
We have not been chosen
to lay the burden down
here. Beneath our feet, the scroll
wraps around
again to *bereshit*. It's the first day
of school, roll is being
called and we are accountable
for what the teacher marks
beside our names: present, absent.

Israel: The Minister of Absorption

You must wait
for the bus to the development

town where you will dwell
if you wish to live

rather than languish
in the myth Jerusalem

I am your friend   I am
history the minister of absorption

[43]

Let me lead you
from the bus of your birth

Here is a beautiful alphabet
Here your identity

card your manna
Here your chair in the desert

Dissolve

By the time you have achieved
    fluency, the woman
        with whom you have longed to

converse has flown
    to the diaspora. By the time
        you can walk without

grief the street on which she lived,
    you have been inducted into the army.
        By the time you can handle

a rifle, she has joined the international peace
    movement. Now
        she campaigns against arms.

By the time your
    arms are strong enough
        to subdue an enemy, carry

a friend from the field,
    she has won
        an award for her first

film, a documentary.
    By the time you get to
        see the film, she has returned

home to care
    for her father, to witness
        the death of Romania

in his bedroom. By the time
    you have learned enough
        about Romania

to be saddened by the death, she
    has become observant, a way
        of combatting

the loneliness of the child
    whose ancestors are now dust
        and smoke.

By the time you have
    mastered the rituals
        of your people, you can no longer

discern where the body ends.
    Now you are one,
        man, woman,

dissolved in the longing
    of mothers and fathers
        to be held, caressed, kissed.

But after first intimacy,
    as she dresses, the weight
        of sleeves, of modernity,

defines her: her body,
    a moment ago, seemed like a river
        of light out of Eden.

Correspondence

A woman who lost a son to the Land
Writes letters daily to the Land.
She addresses the envelope to the Land
With no return address. She lives
At No Return Address where she waits
For the Land to return her son.
Her letters reach the Land
Of Dead Letters and lie in a box
With letters from other mothers
Of No Return Address. When the box is full,
The letters are burned to empty the box
For new letters. Even if the Land could write,
What would it write to the woman who lost her son?
So many mothers have lost children to the Land.
The Land attends to children
Who find their way home. For the children
Of the Diaspora, it has no time.
The Diaspora must care for them, protect them
From the Land that has taken in
The children of so many women
Who devote their lives to composing
Letters to which they receive no reply.

Daughter of Zion

Glory of ancient days
Our salvation, our only hope

Who has she to thank
for making her late for therapy?

There, in the office strewn
with history, she recalls

her first love: *A psalm*
I gave him, a hole

deep enough to fill
with his capacious love.

The therapist does not look up.
Father's gone, and in Miami

now uncle, the last survivor, is dying
to hold her hand before he goes.

He lifts his eyes, the doctor,
and regards his patient

as if she were the end of war,
her dress illuminated

by flames, the face of Sabbath
in her palms.

Israel: Founding Father

Alone at dusk in the orchard
with almond blossoms and gaps

in his long memory—whole years
marked solely by public events,

his private life, during those black
periods, lost somewhere inside him—,

his body stumbles, his soul lurches.
When the soul flies, the body will

clutch the earth, the earth
he now regards, this man who has been

assigned to it, as if from afar,
as if from the Diaspora.

Revelation

Though there is no cure, he seeks one
In the discussions of the rabbis, in the shade
Of the eucalyptus, in the bones of St. Peter fish,
In the lyrics of Arik Einstein, in Gitanes.
Before sleep, uniform slumped
To the ground, pen capped, letter
To the prime minister sealed, he seeks a cure
In the expansive dark of the desert.
In the coffee house, enchanted by a folk singer.
In the shade of the eucalyptus, daydreaming.
Best to forget the offerings, how much oil and grain,
How many calves, how many pigeons.
Forget where the moon is in its cycle.
When the first set ends, when the shade moves,
He wills to carry the forgetting forward.
He wills to practice forgetting when he laces
His shoe, when he describes a recurring dream
To the prisoner who has a reputation
For his interpretations, when he gazes at a ship
On the horizon, when he wakes to the face
Facing his. This is the first time
He has seen her in morning light. What is the prayer?
She belongs to Christ, he remembers as he strokes
Her breast. He will forget this morning,
Like he forgot yesterday morning, their lying
Together late on a mattress issued by the state.
Though there is no cure, he seeks one
Where he works, in a novel, in the kiss
He receives from a rabbi of infinite patience.
He forgets fringes and his friends who have stepped

Outside for a smoke between sets. He forgets
Which of them has lately become a pacifist,
Which has purchased a ticket for the far east.
He wills to practice forgetting the scent
Of her hair, the taste of her tongue.
Though there is no cure, he seeks one
On the broken temple steps,
He seeks one in the morning light
Which reveals and reveals her face.

Shekinah Visits Jerusalem

Shekinah, whose exile extends from broken
Temple steps to the border of heaven and earth,

Broods over the ruins of Jerusalem.
Shadow on the Sabbath

Breads—cast by *Shekinah,* who is the veil
Between divine light and human longing, a bride's veil.

Shekinah travels without papers.
She is the beggar's cup, the Jew's frayed shawl,

The lugubrious cello in the empty concert hall.
In Independence Park, a temporary resident

Bathed in gold, *Shekinah* lies
Until another vagrant, in whose spot she dreams,

Chases her away to wander
The marketplace closing down, afternoon

Of the sixth day, the fruit
Stalls barren now save for one bruised

Pomegranate which she savors, its tart seeds.

IV. from the *Elul* Notebooks

from the *Elul* Notebooks
of Miriam Neviah

In the kitchen, I read
the calendar above the sink:
the blank squares ahead:
    days of awe.

Some months
invite one to live
multiple lives
    at once,

but during *Elul*,
I have no daughter,
no son, no dog,
    no religion.

I am no one's
wife, mother, or friend:
estranged
    by devotion.

    *

But I love my transgressions.
I list them with my new fountain pen.

I glide across the page like a skater,
I hold mother's hand, her new friend's hand

and around the rink we go
(while down the page my sins fall like black snow)

mother whose pockets I am forbidden to explore,
her friend who wishes to build me up like a bridge

to span the river between them,
but I refuse, I let go and am not sorry

when she uses her toe to stop and turns
to retrieve me from the ice that burns

my cheek, not sorry at all to see him tall
above us, above and apart from our small

world, mother and daughter, black glove and mitten.

        *

In the beginning, there was the Father.
But just now when I looked up

from my face afloat on still water
and replied *yes, here I am,*

I knew I had spoken to Pine
Barrens. Once, I would have hanged

rather than find myself here
with His other daughters:

deer, cranberry mist, cedar.
Now I see it's my nature. I hear

with my whole body. Even He cannot
reassure me with His stern comfort

that when I turn from this earth,
I will find mercy, always

beyond the deepest forest I can imagine.
Today my body is the change

of seasons: pumpkin-rust and gourd.
My toe is Goshen Pond. My soul

the flock of geese honking south.

✲

Now I see a skull
floating on the surface
of the water. Because

I drowned people,
others drowned me.
I look away from the blue-

green water, the moral
floating there, and into the book
of repentance, looking for my face

among the beautiful
faces, but the river
winds through me, a shiver

as I spoon
soup into my mouth,
into my child's mouth.

When he refuses
more, I force my love
into him, awful

meal on which he'll grow.

    *

Tonight my beloved
    is mine. He spoils me
with cream and fragrant

oils. He reads to me
    in bed, charms me
with a tale of a demon

luring a boy from the study-
    house to play
by a Gypsy girl's fire.

I know her mother,
    the newsprint-
texture of her breasts, I know

her cousins who spread
    through the woods
like spilled ink.

I am that fire, that girl,
    that demon luring him
into the trap of my tale.

    *

With the help of the Lord,
    my brother

believes he can give birth
    to a child, a nation,

a holy corporation. What need
    has he forsaken

to devote his imagination
    to this exclusive task?

He did not attend
    the birth of his only

sister's child. What can he know
    of the deep bone

strength required
    to endure the slow

thaw, the breaking apart
    of the body, that

glacial mass, all to force
    truth out into daylight

that a mother might
    behold its ruddy face?

He claims to be
    the prophet in this house,

but it is I who have carried
    the weight of the future

inside me, delivered it, cut
    the cord by which it was bound

to a pharaonic past, no matter
    how it displeased me

to see my life
    cancelled in its eyes.

My brother, my brother
    who can hardly speak

for himself, who relies
    on wind

to express his raw rage
    when he finds the tribes,

common laborers, united ·
    in their idling against him.

*

The dog is my cousin.
A bone sustains him.

Aside from the ashen
tip of his tail, he is pure, my chocolate

companion. At dawn
when he hears the shofar, he howls.

Does too much pleasure disturb him?
When he was a boy, my human cousin

lost his family over there.
We were here, not far from here

where my pet, my survivor, comes
when I call. He lies down beside me.

I tweeze the tick hooked behind his ear.
He presses his wet nose to my cheek.

I rub his sternum, making his hind leg
churn as it does when he chases or is chased

by what I can't see beyond our yard.
I keep sharp claws from my sweater.

I fear no harm when we lie together,
side by side, like still waters.

*

My child took a few steps in the yard today.
August, but already first frost was on my mind
As I felt the beating of my ginger heart
And fingered the combs of a poisoned hive.

August, first frost already on my mind.
My wrist ached from a childhood fall
As I fingered the combs of a poisoned hive
And pushed my child higher than reason.

My wrist ached from a childhood fall:
The bike veered away from me.
I pushed my child higher than reason.
For my people, *Elul* is the season to turn inward

Where a bike veers away,
Speeding downhill. I pray hard
For my people. *Elul* is the season to turn toward
Forgiveness, though I cannot forgive

My childhood, speeding down hill, praying hard
Because my father's god is so hard to please.
Nor can I forgive my child. Not quite
A year old, he walks away from me.

Because my father's god is so hard to please,
I learned to live with failure.
A year old and he walks
Toward his own bargain with God.

I learned early to live with failure.
One must labor without expecting love daily.
Toward his own bargain with God
My child labors, stepping, stumbling.

One must labor for love, not expect it daily.
What does he know of the High Holidays?
My child labors, stepping, stumbling.
Horns on the boulevard: warnings.

What will he make of his first High Holidays?
I dream of a loving husband.
Horns on the boulevard: warnings.
My spouse cries out his hunger.

I dream of loving a husband.
Is it our fathers' righteousness that saves us?
My man cries out his hunger
For God, not me, throughout the August night.

Will our fathers' righteousness save us?
The world for my supper, my share.
Somewhere throughout the August night
Lovers perform. My mouth is empty.

The world for my supper, my share.
I feel the beating of my ginger heart.
Lovers perform. My mouth is empty.
My child took a few steps in the yard today.

*

The world is so rich
with its furs in storage
and surf and the nod

from a fellow
commuter on the train
and the mute boy in the park

and William Penn atop
City Hall and steam
from the vendor's beef-

dog cart and a charity
ball to benefit no one
I know, I cannot

relinquish it, not
for an hour of intro-
spection. Let the Lord

inspect me for
imperfections. I'm too
busy examining America's

insects in the park,
modeling an end-of-
season-sale swimsuit

in the mirror. How
I ease my body
into wealth! My ancestors

paid for me
to live without
answering to anyone!

Let Him record
my name in the Book
of Sand, the book

of my tan people
with their tops
down at the Jersey Shore.

       ✻

Last week, I walked with a friend around a lake.
For the first time in public, she wore
her baldness as if it were her soul.
Tossing stones into water, feeding ducks
a stale loaf distracted us for a few minutes,
as did children in the sandbox, on the swings,
until the titter of mothers or sitters turned us
toward the far side of the lake.
For so many years, we were teenagers
sunning in the backyard, swimming in tequila,
dating or terribly alone with faiths that drew us
into increasingly exclusive circles.
How I yearned to kiss her. As we slowly walked,
I held her hand, I held back my tongue.
I hoped the sky would speak.
When our hour was up, my body
and my good name were still one.
Finally at peace, I said this morning
as I dressed her for burial.

✻

Sh'ma Miriam. I close
my eyes and find my place
in the book of the body.
A hot hour before children

are born again in their first
cries from the camp-bus
that drops them at the corner.
Before husband, home

from work, hands me his grief.
For now, love is a good dream
ready to be eaten.
But my back says it has carried

a stranger all day. My breasts
say they are tired of men
who suffer to tame them.
Now hear me, Miriam, says

a heart that knocks, knocks
as if it were locked out
of home. At this hour, summer
laments the harvest and display

of spiral notebook and blunt
pencils, but I am glad to give
my fruit away and turn
to a blank page.

✡

These women I live among, when we meet
at the market, say near the fruit, how they boast

of grandchildren mastering the *alef-bet,* and bleat
of so-and-so's son, a stab in the heart

how he runs, every payday, to craps. They run
a tab for what the Lord owes that one's mother.

Good Jewish boys, what becomes of them!
They grow cold. Blue lines craze my thighs

like your tongue, dear husband, once did.
My breasts may seem weary, but they do not say

let us rest. Now is the time to end your refusal
to kiss me. Lick me. What do you fear?

That you will taste mortality here?
How common we are, women

clipping coupons, denying betrayals we bed with
nightly, alone while our men linger

late over sacred texts.
You are bound to me. Take me now

or forever forfeit my devotion.
Take me away from these bins

spilling over with melons.

*

Because I am not made
a wilderness, my body
tangled with vines and crawling
bugs, a shaft of light
illuminating a trunk
fallen across the path, slowly
rotting, but my skin
is made more fair
in his eyes, my intimacy
perfume and berry
on his lips.
        And he is not
the only one
I've brought my loneliness to
this year, though I favor
his bed for the shrine
to which I bring my prized
offerings.
        Yes, I wear the ring
wherever I am taken,
my whole body
taken into the mouths of strangers
on a linoleum floor, in a bank
vault, before the eyes
of a panting dog. Now
tell me who is the greater fool,
me for believing the covenant
would intensify the pleasure
of betrayal, or you
for taking me
back every morning?

You are righteous, just
and brimming with loving-
kindness. But tonight
I hear you boasting of your power
as I apply eyeliner
and lipstick and dress
to enchant stars.

     ✻

Their hearts are in the east, the far east.
My son's, my daughter-in-law's.

How she savors a plum, the afternoon
gathered around her, the glass

surface of the pool, the brick patio
soft as moss. Perfect posture, she wears

her body like a cotton dress
embroidered with emotions

that do not trouble her chest.
How he repairs the roof: light

in his hand, the hammer.
He is a rare man, his heart

spacious enough to contain
California, the world.

—I couldn't prevent you, Son, from travelling,
nor can I prevent myself from trailing you

to the meditation room where you bow
to a shrine and sit. For the length of my stay,

they give, my son, his bride, their undivided
lives to me, and for the length of my stay

I am not in Philadelphia, lamenting,
lamenting exile. Oh, my soul,

the jasmine luxury of this hour.

　　　*

Is it arrogance that would have me
bury this notebook

along with the other pearls
in the woods you would never dare enter?

You're not interested
in what I treasure. That's why

I leave my notebooks
where I please, this one

open on the desk where you balance
books and I correspond with family.

You know me so deeply, betrayal
is beyond anything you can imagine.

So I am free
to say it here: *I have transgressed.*

Bound by these utterly useless mutterings,
I will never be free of the need

to offer you who cannot hear me
my art, my apology.

        *

Take me, take me
back, *Elul*, month
before the world is born,

before the burning
distance between us
like that between earth

and its nearest star
is created. I am
my beloved's, my beloved is

mine for a moon.
After that, I am turned
away, and belief,

my frail companion, ac-
companies me
from town to town,

wherever I wonder
between sunset and dawn
whether a torn

soul can heal.

What new creation is illuminated
this morning inside me? A mountain

down which water cascades? Praise it.
A scroll concealed in a cave? Praise it.

A tent to shelter all prophesying women?
Praise it, I would praise it.

But the fabric of which mother stitched
a life for me to wear covers my mouth.

My own yard, abuzz with praise
at this time of year, is like a stranger to me

because of mother's envy of everything
that thrives, dies, then before long

thrives once more. If she cannot destroy it
with her love, she'll have nothing

of it, that's her story and why, today, she refuses
to see me. In me she sees the date

of her own demise: my birthday.
In her southern condominium,

she feeds the man who step-fathered me,
each day she feeds him larger portions

of rage against light, the light
that denies her pleasure, never

more than today, eve of the New Year.
My husband's shirt is starched

and perfectly pressed, the table
dressed with apples and honey

for when he returns from prayers with guests.
I invite the world, on the anniversary of its creation,

to enter, to enter me, that I may praise
what dwells within, beyond

the reach of mother's tyranny.

     ✻

Elul has gone, but I am still
here. While I remain behind

to scrape the skillet, the others
gather rewards for having, at last,

before the final blast of the shofar,
fallen to confess personal and collective sins.

Will I be inscribed in the Book of Belatedness?
If you heed these words diligently

you shall have rain and its yield.
In the harvest booth, they string proof:

corn, apple, pomegranate, gourd.
I will rise and recite penitential prayers

only when ready to yield the right
to sin without ceasing for the calendar.

*

When I was a girl, stepfather
trained me to hear no secrets

whispered in the reeds,
no shrieks in the laurel.

How I defied him, giving myself
to willow, sparrow, rain—

all the chattering gods.
Today, first anniversary

of his death, his eyes
no longer contain

what blazed, his final days, everywhere:
blades of grass, girders, my dark art.

Because a Jew is not born
until she sees the Lord

is One, I must be dead, too.
—God, tormentor—what

shall we call Him now?
I am prepared to sacrifice

my art if that is what it takes
to cleave, father, at last, to you.

✵

I love *Elul*. I list my transgressions
then lift my eyes to the mountain.

I love living here, suspended
between the past and redemption.

When I have had enough of vice, I ease
back into the strange goodness my God

expects of me, though even now writing
charity, the pen drags my arm behind it

like a child refusing to go where it must go.
And the children cry, *have mercy on us, answer us.*

To which I reply, I reply,
though your father has abandoned you,

I will take you into the land of Hebrew letters.
But when I am immobile, will you

trouble to load me into a car
and transport me to the river?

Will you help divest my pocket
of the last crumbs of sin?

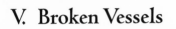

V. Broken Vessels

To Proclaim at Daybreak
Your Steadfast Love

before we are even sure of nearest things—
where, legs folded beneath them, the glasses rest,

and where flung shoes of last night landed, and how
this mule of a body huffed it home, upstairs

and onto the mattress, and whose shape, still plumping
the comforter we've just shed, that is—

let alone things deep, mysterious, or merely strange—
tread of voice in the garden, the neutrino.

At such an hour the jaw hinge is stiff, the tongue leaden.
In its shell, the yolk is a moon; cracking the shell

the knife is a club meeting a skull.
We've been here, flower stuffed into a muzzle

aimed at dissent. Before You have a chance
to fire, we blossom: *a psalm*

for the sabbath day
to proclaim at daybreak Your love steadfast.

No Music

The rabbi tells us music on the Sabbath
is prohibited. No clarinet chuckling
after roast chicken, no accordion
ordering us up on our feet to dance, no fiddle
to delight even the deaf among us.
On the Sabbath, the rabbi says, you shall have
no music, recorded or live, other than that
which can be made without instrumentation,
and he strums the air to illustrate how
to play on this day God ceased from creation.
Not to worry, the rabbi instructs us, not to
disturb the strict peace of the sanctuary
we enter on the Sabbath and from which we depart
wedded, once more, to souls
we divorce and divorce. No gossip, the rabbi
implores, shall pour from the spigots of your mouths,
not on the Sabbath, not on any one of the six
days of the week. But the days leave us weak,
that's why we plead with him to deal with us
mercifully, to give us our *klezmer* and soul, the salve
of Aretha's voice to relieve the pain, the *freylach*
to free us to move back into our bodies, our luxury,
from which we have been exiled too long, our hips,
our buttocks and breasts and the bones of our bones,
but the rabbi says, the rabbi who speaks
from the past where he believes we lived
as our true selves, the redheaded rabbi whose garbled
sermons must make sense to angels, the freckled

rabbi whose long, muscular legs carry him far
from house to house where he inspects the angles
at which *mezuzahs* are hung, the rabbi says no
music on the Sabbath and don't come late to synagogue.

Departure of the Sabbath Queen

At the hour of the Queen's departure, they dance
To the music of American masters
Who return, note by note, the century

Of their birth, its atonality,
Its atoms, its refugees, the spears
Of grass and anonymous lovers

With whom, on leisurely afternoons, they lay
For this is what the musicians would like the Queen to take
With her as she ascends beyond the rafters,

Beyond the roof of the known
Universe, this innovation, this shame
By which the band is shaken into even more

Frenzied playing, amplified
To reach the limits of the city
Within each dancer, faces ablaze

With a refining fire, as the rockers of this
Yeshiva purify themselves in the presence
Of the Queen whose countenance is peace

And whose departure is imminent—the tension
Mounts as they present her, through song, with shorn
Hair and leaky rafts and makeshift sanctuaries

And final calls of vanished species, turning
In two chaste circles, the dancing men and women,
Improvising a post-psalm, the musicians

Who to their maker's laws have returned.

The Well

Not all the poems will be set in Israel in the end.
My pen will drink from the American well in the end.

In the desert my ancestors were guided by smoke and fire.
From atop City Hall, William Penn has me under his spell in the end.

What began with begging to be heard in English,
Has come to whispering up the stairwell in the end.

The bedrooms are dark, the children asleep.
Their dreams will be swept away by the real in the end.

My lamp is their inheritance. My heart, too.
They'll hear its fond farewell in the end.

In the beginning, I created a material world.
The rabbi gave it a soul in the end.

In my coffin, my heart, a little bag of soil.
Dying in the Diaspora turned out swell in the end.

Their poems are being written, the children's, as I speak.
It's the way we make a home of exile in the end.

Though *Torah* was spoken nightly at our table, He never appeared
Who had promised to share our meal in the end.

The bus ride to center city is short, safe and cheap.
Not so the journey underground to Israel in the end.

In the beginning, a slap startled the hand that delivered it.
To fill the hole, they used the back of the shovel in the end.

The year recycles endlessly, but I am never renewed.
I wear the same shroud to crawl or sail in in the end.

I came to the fortune teller to receive the future.
It is they, my foes and enemies, who fall in the end!

Not all the poems need be set in Israel. Wherever we travel,
Our poems will accompany us like Miriam's Well in the end.

I and Thou: Can't Get Over You

After returning from Jerusalem, I visited
    the Emporium.
At first I used that field-glass part of my brain
    to view them from a distance:
women beaming from glass cages.
    Shyness came and disappeared—maybe
it was shame—, but soon enough my background
    shrunk from substance
and fullness leaving me free to be
    what I was: a functional point.
I can't say how, in the end, I chose
    to take possession of the particular woman
I chose, but the latched door with its red light
    signalled to the other assembled loners: stay away.

Jerusalem, they say, is a cave
    of light bursting the bonds of vessels
created to contain it. One day I gave up that mysticism.
    The next, I stood alone, a network of impulses
in a plywood closet large enough
    for an adventurous couple.
Her features, magnified by the lens of my longing
    for contact, let themselves be taken
but did not give themselves to me.
    It was my first day home. I needed density, duration.
She stuck her finger in there, I stuck
    my finger in here.   I can't quite express
what she said to me with her ass, but I knew if I should die in it
    my grave would be in nothingness.

Therapy

There is no time in this room.
No weather, no glass of grammar.
No rabbi waiting to catch you, no song
    to tie us to the ottoman
on which my infidelity first brushed
    against yours.

My license is over there, my vacation over
there, the light in my eye is over there,
the shadow of one of my best ideas over there

    when you are here.

When you are here, you are
    the water I drink,
the cotton against my loneliness,
    the tower of it.

I don't care what my blouse says.

This is the most practical advice I can offer.
Talk to me. Talk to me. Talk
    to me forever, for an hour every two weeks.

When your family is in my ear,
your wife's mood on my pad,
I have almost enough of you.

I have almost enough of you

when your poem is inside me.
When the ground is under me.
When the 24 moods of me-under-you
    are printed.

This is practical. I can live without television
    when your story is on me.

There is no marriage in the county
that has not opened its window
to let out the smoke, let in the honeysuckle,

no judge who has not felt green under the robe,
no street that has not told me its dream
    of becoming a wall,
no wall that has not told me its dream
    of becoming a river,
no dollar that has not, at last, revealed
    its hiding place.

I know what your birthday says about the way you unwrap,
I know what my hair says when you are near, far.
I want you to keep my hair in a private place.

I know that my husband's dark lamp
meditates in the next room, his office,
    while you are here.

There is no medication in my falling
    to your tongue.
There is no map on which you can locate me
    when I am gone into your hand.

I Know What Happiness Is

In the morning I stand at the sink, I sink my face
Into the bowl of my hands, and I look for you
At the bottom of the bowl.
I drive the road into town, I drive the road out of town,
I turn the wheel and turn the wheel and in the wheel's
Turning, I look for you.
The stars were overhead when I was born.
The stars are overhead now. This must be the hour
   of your birth.
Why do I feel so alone? No one misses me
When I am among them at the party.
She does not dance with me when I dance with her
   at the party,
Because whether I'm dancing or chatting with the others
At the party, I'm missing because I'm out looking for you.
The years, the years go by and little happens.
I am paid and I pay others. I am loved and I love others.
I look for you and not much happens.
One afternoon I lay near a pond and smoked a joint.
The ground on which I lay opened and I fell in
And the ground closed over me. I was happy there
But the feeling passed. I looked for you to tell you
I know what happiness is. You must be so close
I can't see you. I must be looking right at you.
When it rains, I am content
To read, though I look up every page or two to see
If you are near. When I want to feel lonely, I look for you.
When I want to look for you, I distract myself. Look,
One of the bulbs in the chandelier needs to be replaced.

When everyone I know joins me
In looking for you, I continue looking as hard as I always have
Or at least I look as if I'm looking hard for you.
There is no end to this. If one day you should say, *Son, I am here,*
I would answer, *Yes, here we are, together,* and go on looking for you.

Broken Vessels

I. *Keter (Crown)*

This is the way we prefer the baby to be born, luminous
Void first, trailed by the crown, the body
Falling like an astronaut from the *without end*
Into the kingdom of forms, until he splashes
Down in his mother's palms, the afterglow
Of a shattered essence.

II. *Tiferet (Beauty)*

Here
On formal days he is ten syllables
And on others, when he's feeling rambunctious or
Free, he is
As long or short as he needs to be.

In the mountains, he discovers the beauty of centering,
Of practicing stillness, of letting
The trail, light, weather, poem
Pass through him, seeking
A place to rest, a summit on which to build,
From the top up, a new kingdom.

III. *Malkhut (Kingdom)*

If you were invited to settle here, would you?
How long before you would feel
Incomplete without the endlessness of the poem

Which one cannot even imagine?
But he has imagined it, encircling him
Wherever he steps, even here
As he climbs
The ladder of longing
Toward the source of light illuminating this page.

Rosh Hashanah

On this day a slow but wise King
At the palace window surveys his kingdom.
Our souls fly to meet their father.
Abandoned, our bodies converse with pigeons
And rivers, ticks and stones: their souls
Have also flown to appear before their father.
As pure today as they were ten thousand years ago,
The souls float on a river of divine light
And do not interest him. He desires
Our bodies—scarred, bent, wired, pierced, singed . . .
He examines the surfaces on which we walk,
Measures the walls against which we're thrown,
Weighs the air we breathe, samples the water
In which we bathe.

       The rest of the year he pities
Those souls. Today he rubs the bodies, fills the eyes
With beauty, tickles the ears with truth, he touches the toes
Of a man who has smoked for a hundred years
And the belly of a baby who glows with milk,
Forgetting not the crab or rat or beetle or moth,
Not the oak or phlox flickering on the side of the road.

Yom Kippur 5759

My groaning serves as my bread.
My rising serves as my falling.

I have floated all year. I have
feasted and rested while the wind

fluttered the sleeves of the thin
and the moon lifted the faces

of the pale who sounded
their hollow O above my dream.

Now my trembling serves as my grooming:
I groom for an audience with you.

My listening serves as my calling,
my reply to you as my contrition:

Here am I. Here am I.

My turning serves as my awakening,
my turning of pages, of pages:

surely you will pass by, the shadow
of your wrath will glide

over the curled boy
without troubling his wakeful reading.

My searching serves as my roaring.
It pours forth as water, it cascades.

I bend inside my rebelling (my way
of knowing) and stand inside my pleading:

Lord, grant me this,
this cold yearning, this burning vow:

Let me live to serve.

Even as the green outside is slowing,
my standing serves as my going.

Psalm

Somewhere a man is writing a psalm.
Maybe it's late, his child
sleeping under dreams,
his wife coughing, shivering, spitting,
touching a clock on the bedside table.
Let's say they have lived on just enough
hope for many years, let's say one day
God's not a bad idea.

Maybe the man fixes cars
for a living, I don't know,
I can't ask him right now, maybe
he assists a teacher in the local school,
maybe he's a prosecutor, a defender.
I don't want to disturb him; he's earned
this solitude, he'll pay for it.

He is lucky, he thinks
as he waits at the table, late at night,
for the next verse
of the psalm he's composing.
Just before worming under the covers,
his son laid out tomorrow's uniform.
His wife, before the syrup
quieted her, scribbled a note
to herself. She's certain
the floor will be there at dawn
when her feet fall from bed.

The psalm? I can't read it
from here, it's cupped in his hand.
Let it be a psalm of praise,
praise the roof that keeps them
dry, praise the farmer, picker, packager,
shipper, stocker, checker, bagger, wife—
the network by which he is fed,
praise the doctor who examines
and assures him, this father, husband,
worker, worrier, that it's nothing,
praise the sleeplessness that gives him
these quiet hours, this yellow pad,
and a fan to draw relief into the August house.

Notes

page 11: *Elul:* The sixth month in the religious calendar and the twelfth and last in the civil year. It has twenty-nine days and typically falls in August or September. As *Elul* is the month preceding Rosh Hashanah and Yom Kippur, it is a month of repentance and spiritual preparation.

page 15: *shofar:* a ram's horn blown during worship services on the Jewish high holidays and throughout the month of *Elul.* Its blast is a reminder to repent.

page 41: *Adonai-Yireh:* "And Abraham named that site [where a ram was offered instead of Isaac] Adonai-yireh [the Lord will see], whence the present saying 'On the mount of the Lord there is vision'" (*Gen.* 22:14).

page 42: *Sivan:* The ninth month of the civil year and the third month of the religious year. The month during which the festival of *Shavuot,* which marks the anniversary of the giving of the Torah, is celebrated.

page 43: *Bereshit:* The first word of the Torah. Translated as "In the beginning."

page 52: *Shekinah:* The name of the feminine aspect of God. Translated as "indwelling presence."

page 68: *Sh'ma Miriam:* Hear, O Miriam. The phrase plays off *Sh'ma Yisrael,* the first words of the prayer in which Jews declare their belief in the oneness of God.

page 69: *alef-bet:* The first two letters of the Hebrew alphabet.

page 82: *freylach:* In Klezmer music, *freylach* is a joyous melody or song.

page 83: *mezuzah:* A small, rectangular box affixed to doorposts of Jewish homes. It contains a parchment inscribed with the *sh'ma* prayer.

page 84: *yeshiva:* A Jewish rabbinical seminary.

page 93: *Keter, Tiferet, Malkhut:* Three of the ten vessels of creation, according to Kabbalistic cosmology.

Acknowledgments

The author gratefully acknowledges the editors and publishers of the journals and anthologies where some of the poems in this collection first appeared, often in different form.

Journals

Ascent: "from the *Elul* Notebooks of Miriam Neviah: But I love my transgressions" (formerly entitled "Miriam's Cheek Burns"), "*Leviticus* for Daughters"

Bellingham Review: "*Shekinah* Visits Jerusalem" (formerly entitled "*Shekinah*")

Crab Orchard Review: "Klezmer"

Denver Quarterly: "Way Down"

Judaism: "Home" and "Israel: Founding Father" (formerly entitled "Founding Fathers")

Kenyon Review: "Broken Vessels"

Kerem: "Departure of the Sabbath Queen"

New England Review and Bread Loaf Quarterly: "Dissolve"

N. C. Crossroads: Publication of the North Carolina Humanities Council: "Yom Kippur 5759"

North Carolina Literary Review: "from the *Elul* Notebooks of Miriam Neviah: In the beginning, there was the Father" (formerly entitled "Miriam: Pine Barrens")

Prairie Schooner: "Desert Crossing: First Day" (formerly entitled "First Day"), "Correspondence," "Abortion"(formerly entitled "*I and Thou:* Abortion")

Tampa Review: "I Know What Happiness Is," "Therapy," "Meditation upon Waking in *Elul*," "Psalm"

TriQuarterly: "Revelation"

Anthologies:

Ravishing DisUnities: an Anthology of Real Ghazals (Wesleyan University Press, 2000): "The Well."

The Sacred Place: Witnessing the Holy in the Physical World (University of Utah Press, 1996): "Rosh Hashanah"

Telling and Remembering: A Century of American Jewish Poetry (Beacon, 1997): "No Music"

For their generous and wise counsel on the poems in this book and for their unwavering support, I would like to thank Don Morrill, Lisa Birnbaum, Shirley Kaufman, Alan Shapiro, Rodger Kamenetz, Amanda Schaffer, Robin Behn, Robin Hemley, and Rebecca McClanahan. A special thanks to Richard Mathews, visionary publisher, patient editor, kind man.

Richard Chess is an associate professor of literature and language at the University of North Carolina at Asheville. He directs UNCA's Center for Jewish Studies. His first book of poetry, *Tekiah*, appeared in the University of Georgia's Contemporary Poetry Series in 1994. His poems have been anthologized in *Telling and Remembering: A Century of American-Jewish Poetry* (Beacon, 1997), *The Sacred Place: Witnessing the Holy in the Physical World* (Utah, 1996), and *Ravishing DisUnities: An Anthology of Real Ghazals* (Wesleyan, 2000). His poems have also been published widely in journals including *Tampa Review, Prairie Schooner, Crab Orchard Review, Kenyon Review, TriQuarterly*, and others.